A LAKE OF LIGHT AND CLOUDS

Also by Terri Kirby Erickson

Thread Count
Telling Tales of Dusk
In the Palms of Angels

A Lake of Light
and Clouds

Poems

Terri Kirby Erickson

Press 53
Winston-Salem

Press 53
PO Box 30314
Winston-Salem, NC 27130

First Edition

Cover design by Kevin Morgan Watson

Cover art, "A Lake of Light and Clouds," Copyright © 2014 by Stephen White

Cover art photograph by J. Sinclair Photography

Biography page author photo by Jan G. Hensley

Back cover author photo by Superieur Photographics

Printed on acid-free paper

ISBN 978-1-941209-02-8

For Gia, my flower child

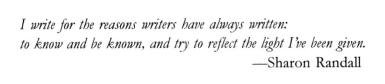

I write for the reasons writers have always written:
to know and be known, and try to reflect the light I've been given.
—Sharon Randall

ACKNOWLEGMENTS

Many thanks to the editors of the following publications where these poems (and in a few cases, earlier versions of these poems) first appeared:

2013 Poet's Market: "At the Bowling Alley"
27 rue de fleures: "Stevie Santos"
...And Love (Jacar Press Anthology): "Frank and Alice: A Love Story"
Boston Literary Magazine: "Hospital Parking Lot"
Carolina Woman Magazine: "Searching for Scallop Shells," "Kenmore"
Dead Mule School of Southern Literature: "At the Waffle House," "Making Cornbread," "Agnes"
Foundling Review: "7-Eleven"
Green Briar Review: "Sixteen," "Palmist"
Hektoen International: "After the Funeral"
Muse India: "Orange Butterfly," "Fox"
Nazim Hikmet Poetry Competition Chapbook: "Blind," "Battered," "Nannie White"
Old Mountain Press Anthologies: "Ants," "High Country Winter," "Irises"
Pinesong: "Frank and Alice: A Love Story"
Pirene's Fountain: "Shapeshifting," "Woman on the Dock," "The Man Who Cuts His Grass with Nail Scissors"
Poems with Heart Charity Project Anthology: "Flower Child"
Poetica Magazine: "Shabbat Elevator"
Red River Review: "Pool Shark," "The Dirt Road"
Scythe: "At the Urologist's Office"
storySouth: "Red Tractor," "Loretta Wray"
Tapestry, Issue No. 25: "Zora-May Pettigrew"
The Rusty Nail: "Vincenzos," "Rose"
Time of Singing: "Bluebird," "Blackbird"
vox poetica: "Trash Man"
Wilmington Star News (Port City Poets): "Angels of Death"

Award-winning Poems:

"Orchid," Winner, "Poetry for their Freedom" contest, sponsored by the Center for Women and Where Writers Win, in support of the U.S. East Coast office of the A21 Campaign, with the theme, "The Crime of Human Trafficking and the Hope and Restoration of Victims," 2013

"Kenmore," Grand Prize Winner, *Carolina Woman* Writing Contest, 2013

"Dust," Finalist, Randall Jarrell Poetry Competition, 2013

"How to Sing the Blues," Finalist, Rita Dove Poetry Award, Salem College International Literary Awards, 2012

"Bluebird," Editor's Choice, *Time of Singing* Summer Poetry Contest, 2012

"Blackbird," Second Place, *Time of Singing* Summer Poetry Contest, 2012

"Searching for Scallop Shells," Honorable Mention, *Carolina Woman* Writing Contest, 2012

"At the Bowling Alley," Honorable Mention, Randall Jarrell Poetry Competition, 2011

"Blind," "Battered," "Nannie White," Winners/Finalists of the International Nazim Hikmet Poetry Competition, 2011

"Frank and Alice: A Love Story," First Place, Poetry of Love Award, North Carolina Poetry Society, 2011

"Angels of Death," First Place, Poetry Contest, Port City Poets, *Wilmington Star News*, 2009; set to music as part of a song cycle by composer Theodore Wiprud, 2013

A Lake of Light and Clouds

I.

II.

III.

IV.

V.

VI.

I

Red Tractor

Just before you reach the Triple B Country
Sausage sign, there's an old red tractor
hunkering down beside the road.

You can hear the heavy sighs as it nestles
into the leaves, loosening its belt
and letting its chassis hang low. Blink

and you'll miss it twitch like a sleeping dog—
the rise and fall of its rust-covered ribs
when it rolls at last, into a dream of wheat.

LORETTA WRAY

My mother, lipstick red, barefoot, toenails painted
the palest shade of pink, stretched out her dancer's legs
and rubbed suntan lotion into a face
that should have been magnified on a movie screen—
the kind that bowled men over even with curlers in her hair
and children dangling from both hands wherever she went.
They never saw the greasy chaise lounge behind our house
where the sun whispered sonnets in her ears
and darkened her skin with hot kisses while the radio
played "Blue Velvet." And the green grocer and the mailman
and the gas station attendants and the jean-clad
teenage boys loitering downtown on Saturday afternoons,
who caught glimpses of Loretta Wray every now
and then, if they were lucky, would have dropped dead with desire
if they'd seen her sunning herself in our backyard wearing
nothing but a two-piece bathing suit and a lazy, sun-drenched
grin, the best years of her life almost, but not quite, past.

FRANK AND ALICE: A LOVE STORY

In the crowded confines of a noisy
newsroom, foreheads crease in concentration
over coffee-stained keyboards as story
after story is recorded, clack, clack, clack

with clerical precision. Phones cradled
on cricked shoulders feed "quotes"

to the eager ears of frenzied reporters
needing more substance to *flesh out* the skeletal
skittering of clipped sentences
glaring on their computer screens.

Fresh-faced, pencil-thin young women
snack on fat-free yogurt and granola bars

while wrinkled old curmudgeons munch
three-day-old doughnuts.

And then there's Frank with his neat
containers of perfectly balanced meals, lovingly
prepared by his wife, whose nightly call
sends him into paroxysms

of astonished delight as if he can't quite
believe his great good fortune of being the only
man in the whole world lucky enough
to marry Alice.

Sixteen

The boy next door has spray-painted the words
Ole Blue on the tailgate of his pickup truck,
the one his grandfather gave him that sounds
like a space shuttle firing up when he turns the key.
It will rock him in its blue arms for as long as boys
will drive a vehicle that only other boys like.
Girls prefer a newer model that doesn't cough
and sputter like an old man on a cold morning—
with plush seats and lighted mirror on the visor.
But the boy doesn't care right now what they think.
When he opens the door that creaks like the entrance
to a haunted house and slides into a seat warmed
already, by the memory of his grandfather's denim
haunches, his life is perfect and made more perfect
when he and *Ole Blue* are cruising down a country road,
radio playing, one sunburned arm lying across the track
of his open window—the other spinning a wheel
that lands him every time on lucky sixteen.

GRASSHOPPERS

Today the field is full of grasshoppers.
It looks as if the grass has left its roots behind,
joyfully jumping—each blade reveling
in its new-found freedom, propelling itself
from the place to which it has long been fettered,
as close as possible to the sky.

There, the tatted lace clouds are ripping
themselves from their blue bindings, racing
over trees shaking their heads at such foolishness,
though shrubs and saplings swing and sway,
eager to join the dance.

Everything's in motion, even the miniature ponies,
fine with leaning against each other like fence
posts all winter, are trotting around
in circles, their sharp little hooves leaving holes
in the ground like women wearing stilettos—
their breath scented with wild strawberry

and white clover. Meanwhile, the grasshoppers,
which can leap twenty times their bodies' length,
are still on the move, mandibles packed
with brown juice like baseball players chewing
tobacco, legs quivering from the hard

work of lifting from one side of the field
to the other, a creature that wears its skeleton
on the outside like a coat, eats more than a cow
will in a single day—but can also jump,
resembling tiny puffs of green air—as if the earth
in spring is so content, it can't stop sighing.

AT THE BOWLING ALLEY

Blind, the old man still beats you. He holds
the heavy ball as if it's made of Styrofoam, pitches
it down the alley and stands there, listening for
the strike. You marvel that this dreg of humanity
with his hawk-nosed face and unwashed body,
tattoos dripping down the slack skin of his arms
and between the lizard-like folds of his scrawny
neck, wins every game. The fact that he's blind,
too, is the final insult since you can spot a fly
circling a cup of greasy French fries from across
the dang building—the barrettes in Missy Cardwell's
curly blonde hair as she's walking to the restroom
at the far-end of the hall, her short skirt swinging
from side to side in that flirty way of hers that drives
you half-crazy. Maybe that's it—the old man has no
distractions. There's nothing but the feel of the ball
in his hands, the squeak of his beat-up bowling shoes
on the polished floor, and the sound of ten pins knocked
down in one fell swoop, hit so hard you wonder if
they'll ever get up. And even worse, he's your father,
the same sorry guy who took off when you were six.
You know he knows who you are, but he never
says a word—just whips the living fool out of you
and walks away, as if you're just another loser.

Hospital Parking Lot

Headscarf fluttering in the wind,
stockings hanging loose on her vein-roped
legs, an old woman clings to her husband

as if he were the last tree standing in a storm,
though he is not the strong one.

His skin is translucent—more like a window
than a shade. Without a shirt and coat,

we could see his lungs swell and shrink,
his heart skip. But he has offered her his arm,
and for sixty years, she has taken it.

The *Star*

for Ron Powers

In Hannibal, Missouri, the Mississippi River
could lure a boy from his bed come Saturday
morning, teeming as it was with fish just waiting
to be caught and bathwater-warm in summer,
perfect for a swim. Its murkier secrets rarely rose
above a whisper—so softly spoken they might
have been waves lapping the jagged shoreline,
but Hannibal boys could hear them loud and clear—
and most came running. Still, when afternoon rolled
around, every boy with a nickel headed straight
for the *Star*, pushing and shoving for the best seats
to the matinee, pockets stuffed with river rocks,
leftover bait, gum wrappers and just enough
money to get in. For the next two hours, they'd sit
with friends and even deadly enemies—the bullies
and freeloaders among them always looking
for a fight or a handout—in a bliss of entertainment
for which none of them would trade a single minute.
They were all the same in the dark, anyway, these boys
of every shape and social situation, stout or lean,
rich or poor, destined to grow into their adult lives
as good citizens or bad. None of that mattered once
the houselights dimmed and they hunkered down
in their seats, bathed in a kind of phosphorescent
glow from the big screen, faces filled with awe
and wonder. They cheered when their movie heroes,
tangling with one foe after the other, came out on top—
became so caught up in the story that even after the film
was over, they swaggered through the exit and down
Main Street—Jujubes stuck to the soles of their shoes—
like a pack of gunslingers turned sheriffs who saved

the town and married the prettiest girls. They pretended
not to care about girls at all—mystical creatures as filled
with dark promise as the Mississippi. But there was plenty
of time to worry about women and only so many hours
left to be a boy with nothing better to do than spend
Saturday mornings flinging homemade fishhooks
and their lithe, young bodies into the river, and every
Saturday afternoon watching Hollywood find its way
to Hannibal, Missouri, and the *Star*.

BLUEBIRD

Light as crumbs on a plate,
a bluebird perched on the porch

railing, cocking its head this way
and that, feathers

the indigo blue of a king's hand-
dyed robe, or the sky

on its bluest day, drained of clouds
and concentrated in the bottom

of God's drinking glass, which He
swirled and swallowed,

then breathed out this little bird,
now flying.

THE MILL HOUSE

At the Mill House the sound of a waterwheel
turning is as soothing as your mother's voice
when you were fretful in your crib and she,
leaning over it, sang to you. It is a home
now—no longer grinding grain into flour—
but a great stone manse beside a lake of light
and clouds, with willows on the banks that dip
and sway together with their mirrored partners.
On fine days, we sometimes see the owners'
children on the weathered dock, setting free
the tethered paddleboats shaped like swans—
their hands small and luminous against the
folded, fiberglass wings, the graceful curve
of a swan's white neck. Far away the world
still whirs and shakes, bellows and bugles its
wretched roar over lands scarred by burning
buildings and bodies left lying where they
have fallen. But here, the wheel spins slowly
and swan boats circle the man-made lake—
carrying boys and girls so lovely, so fragile,
if you touch them they might turn to dust.

II

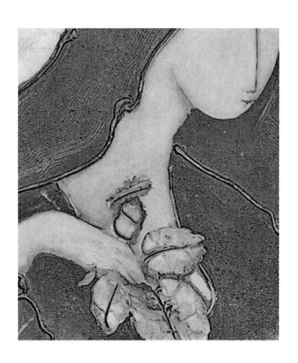

FLOWER CHILD

Flower child, where did you come from?
Your hands are bigger than mine, stronger.
They are seldom still. Digging in the dirt, stringing beads
on a necklace, snapping your fingers to a Beatles song—
you are always moving forward, dragging the past
behind you like a streamer. You are happier barefoot,
dancing in the grass, than women
wearing designer shoes, jumping in a pile of money.
Pierced and tattooed, silver bracelets jingling,
you are as different from me as *North*
is to *South*. Yet wherever you go, my heart,
like the needle on a compass, follows.

KENMORE

The Kenmore range tried to make friends
with the other appliances, but the refrigerator
gave her the cold shoulder. Besides, he hummed
all the time and his breath smelled like moldy
cheese. The microwave made her jump when
he said *ding*, and his face was always dirty—
smeared with exploded eggs and bits of hotdog.
The can opener poked her nose into everybody's
business and the toaster had a crummy personality,
so making friends with them was out. That left
the dishwasher, who foamed at the mouth like
a rabid dog whenever he cleaned the dishes.
She wished the washing machine and dryer—
such a nice, quiet couple—lived closer, but they
were in the basement, a dark, dank place the owner
hardly ever visited. He seldom cooked a real meal,
either, so the range sat idle, mourning the house
from where she was recently removed, making
way for the newest model. She tried winking
all four of her eyes at the lonely man who bought
her, but he never noticed—just microwaved
his dinner and took it into the den. She missed
listening to people talk around a kitchen table;
pined for boiling pots and moo-cow oven mitts;
remembered all too well how good her belly felt
when it was full of turkey and rump roast, pork
loin and Cornish hens. Once, she felt needed,
necessary, part of a family. Now she's just
an old stove, cool to the touch, with nothing
but memories to keep her warm.

ORANGE BUTTERFLY

Settling on the ground
like a fallen leaf,
an orange butterfly
mimics the still grass,
its wings pressed
together like the thin
pages of an old book—
then flutters away,
bright as parchment
flared with fire, flying
up a blue chimney.

How to Sing the Blues

Open your mouth for the mute, in the cause
of all who are left desolate.
                    —Proverbs 31:8

Don't hold nothing back, she said, drawing smoke
from a lipstick-stained cigarette deep into her lungs.
You can't be shy on stage because, baby, you are naked
up there. If you ain't, they'll know as soon as you
open your mouth. That's right. You got to lean into
that microphone like it's a man, see, a man who done
you wrong. And you need to tell him about it. You
need to say whatever it takes to bring him back. Remind
him how good it's been, how sweet. It won't be easy.
He's got one foot out the door, his new woman waiting
in the car. And he'll do the same to her some day, as he's
doing to you. But you don't care how bad your man
is. You love him. And the sun won't shine no more
if you can't sing him back to you right here, right now,
and this is your last chance. So open your mouth. Sing
like you never sung before. And do it every time—
not just when you feel like it, or if you got yourself a big
crowd. The first night you don't, leads to the next night
and the next. Before long, you can't find the feeling
even when you're looking for it and, honey, you don't
want that to happen. 'Cause you got it in you to sing
so people taste salt when it's you up there, crying. And
no broke-down blues singer, ten steps from the grave,
can tell you nothing you don't know. So go on, now.
Claim the world you're about to own, and if I'm still alive,
give me a call. Tell me what it feels like, to be a star.

7-Eleven

With a vacant look on her too-tired face,
a woman sweeps cigarette butts and cellophane wrappers
into a dustpan, the tips of her yellow hair
swinging back and forth

across a crooked name tag. She is cleaning the filthy
sidewalk in front of a 7-Eleven, a basketball-
size pregnancy bursting the seams
of her pink sweatshirt. Under the harsh glare

of florescent parking lot lights that switched on promptly
at dusk, she looks older than she probably is, her skin
picking up gray tones
from the trash cans nobody bothers to use,

and the gunmetal frame on a cage packed with propane
tanks. Every now and then, the corners of her mouth
turn up so you can see how she might
have looked holding

a glass of lime punch instead of a broom
handle, surrounded by baby gifts and giggling girlfriends
instead of drunks, deadbeats and drifters,
with nothing left to give.

At the Urologist's Office

My husband and I sit side
by side in the sub-zero exam
room. There isn't a country

in the world colder than this.
Penguins would thrive here,
and polar bears. Perusing

anatomically correct charts
on the walls, I'm reminded

of my fifth grade sex education
class—the detailed drawings

of male privates projected
on a pull-down screen—a boy
named Vincent Vanderpool

poking his pencil into my back
each time the teacher pointed

to a body part. If only I could
comprehend what this doctor

is saying. He might as well be
speaking Inuit until the word
cancer rolls off his tongue,

comes hurtling toward us like
a snowball packed around a rock—
too fast for anyone to duck.

FIGHT NIGHT

Back before pay-per-view, a working man
could sit down with a beer and watch the greatest
boxers in the world duke it out for free in his own den—
black and white TV blaring, images flickering in the dark
room where Dad and I hovered near the edge of our chairs
for as long as the fight lasted. You see, my father spent
eight hours a day doing a job he hated, and every evening
slap-worn-out from the effort. But none of that mattered once
Muhammad Ali, George Foreman or Smokin' Joe Frazier jumped
into the ring and, man oh man, you could tell Dad felt the punches
on his own face, the blood and sweat pouring into his eyes,
the cuts swelling. And I was right there beside him—
a pale, skinny kid with glasses, who was always chosen last
for any team sport unless somebody had a broken leg
or was projectile vomiting. With my dad on boxing
night, however, I was one of the guys. Why, the two of us
were practically hanging on the ropes ourselves,
we were that close to being there and even better, my father
was talking to me like I was a grown-up—not some snot-
nosed brat he had to dodge on his way to the refrigerator,
but one of his best friends—maybe the best friend
he ever had, even if I was just his daughter.

CAMEL

Off Highway 46 near Gnawbone, Indiana, a camel feeds
on fescue—the balmy air nothing like the hot, desert
wind that blows such beasts into the world, spitting
and coughing. Cars cruise along the rusted wire fence

that separates the farmer's land from the busy road,
where drivers glimpse, when passing by, an animal
they've never come across before except in pictures.

We marvel at its hairy hump, how the large, lumbering
mammal rolls when it moves, like a ship on a green

sea of grass. Lips protruding in a pout, its toothy
underbite pulls whatever food it finds from the Indiana
soil, the scene so different from the landscape of its

birth. There, the sun burns the infinite sky like fire.
And shifting sand makes mountains overnight, beneath

stars cold as chips of ice chiseled from the moon.
But tomorrow it will wake again to this small pasture,
the sky just a tattered blue cloth hanging from the tree

branches, the ground too firm for feet designed to
cross the dunes. And no creatures of its kind live here,
except in dreams, where a caravan of camels shimmers
in the distance—then fades from view, like a mirage.

BUTTER CHURN

Granny in her good cotton dress and clean apron,
rode the butter churn sidesaddle. Her right hand

worked the cream—her left hand held the churn
steady. Even posing for a picture, she didn't

smile. She was doing her best to make churning
butter in her Sunday clothes, in front of the dirt-

stained kitchen door, the flyswatter hanging from
a nail in the wall, look natural—while my mother,

a girl in pigtails, gazed down at the work in store
for her some day, when Granny's arm gave out.

SHABBAT ELEVATOR

To keep the day holy, the Shabbat elevator
at Mount Sinai Hospital stops on every floor.
It carries you like a father would his sleepy
child. There is nothing for you to do—no buttons
to push, no will of yours that must be exercised.
It takes you where you're going, but not so fast.
The doors will open and close like theater curtains
on floors you never dreamed of visiting, where
patients wearing thin cotton gowns are curled
like hermit crabs in their borrowed beds, harried
nurses hurry from room to room on their silent
soles, and doctors with furrowed foreheads roam
the halls in herds, the young ones tossing medical
terms between them like Frisbees. You might
see rabbis, priests, and preachers; workers pushing
food carts, laundry hampers, trash receptacles,
gurneys; patients' relatives and friends; people
laughing, crying, talkative or quiet, who have traded
their docile ride for whatever scene they waited
just like you, to enter. Soon enough, it will be
your turn to step onstage, to join the cast of a play
already in progress. So rest, relax. Let the story
unfold for a while, without you.

BLIND

A woman, newly blind, has watched the light
fade softly, making a sound like rain.

Once, colors were torrential—
shapes, a downpour. Now the patter of memory

is all she has left—faces of friends, words
on a page, falling

leaves, her own body—all gone from her sight,
all lost in the swirling

fog. She does not cry. Instead, she places her
hands each day, on the life

that she remembers—tender, adoring,
as if it is a lover, sleeping with her in the dark.

LEROY AND VIOLA

Come Saturday morning, poor black men
gathered on street corners, waiting for white
men in Cadillacs to drive by slow, shouting
hey boy from their rolled-down windows, *get
in*, which meant there was a job digging ditches
or other backbreaking work for less money
than it cost to feed the family dog. Nights
were harder, what with hooded gangs of racists
wrapped in bed sheets roaming the countryside,
and woe to anybody who wasn't white once
those half-drunk, hatemongering mobs with
their burning crosses and lengths of rope,
arrived on the scene. So in 1965 when married
mother-of-five Viola Gregg Liuzzo volunteered
to drive nineteen-year-old Leroy Moton back
to Selma—both fresh from a freedom march
in Montgomery, Alabama—the sight of a white
woman with a black man in the front seat of
a vehicle sporting Michigan plates didn't sit
well with Klansmen who were, as usual, wild
as pent-up ponies in a barn blaze. So they chased
the pair down and fired two bullets into Liuzzo's
brain, laughing like loons when the car careened
into a ditch. Covered in blood, Moton played
dead—surviving the shots, the crash, and the killers'
swift perusal of the wreckage. But Viola Liuzzo
is gone except in memory, where the same reel
runs over and over in Leroy Moton's mind:
a pretty woman's profile, pale as milk against
the purpling sky, and his hand, dark as rivers
on the radio dial—strangers joined forever
by history, seconds before the slaughter.

III

POOL SHARK

The door to a dive opens and light washes in like a swell
of seawater, then recedes, leaving behind the pool
shark. His pointy teeth gleam in the glow of bare bulbs
hanging from the low ceiling, so he quickly closes

his trap and waits by a scarred, nicotine-yellow wall,
for the chance to play a game. He brought his own

pool cue and keeps it close, though anyone can see it's
cheaply made and so brand-new he stripped the plastic
off the box in the parking lot. Drunks propped against
the ash-covered plank that serves as a bar, snicker

behind his faux-leather-clad back—call him *sucker*
and other names less flattering, but he ignores them all.

Through the fake lens of wire-rimmed glasses held together
by duct tape—he keeps his eyes on the players until it's
his turn to chalk his tip and toss a few bucks on the burn-

pocked rail. Like the nearsighted nerd he pretends to be,
he misses most of the shots, but makes just enough

to seem lucky sometimes. So the bets go higher and higher
until the final game, when the other guys—a small-time

dealer and a pimp flush with cash—watch gap-mouthed
as the pool shark circles the tired table and runs it clean,
then grabs the stack of greens and disappears faster
than a fin, before anyone can catch him.

SHAPESHIFTING

Next to you in the night, I am as far
from my human self as I ever can be—
uncaring of death, fearless in a way that eludes
me when the sun rises and this nest
of ours is filled with light. Here in the dark, the animal
that rests patiently within me through
the long hours of the day,
begins to stir. For her, nothing matters
but the silk of your skin, the rhythm of your breath,
the heat from our bodies, coupling.
And when sleep finally comes, we slip into it as if sleep
is a kind of water—
and there is no such thing as drowning.

Dust

...for you are dust and to dust you shall return.
—Genesis 3:19

The drought came first, then the dying crops
and after that, dust. It rose from the dry, dead
ground like the fists of an angry god that smote
again and again the land and the living creatures
on it. Cattle fending for themselves suffocated
and birds fell from the sky like stones. People
died of dust pneumonia, starvation, and despair.
Babies born in the midst of it knew nothing but
dust and more dust. Days were dark as nights,
and women hung damp sheets in the windows of
their houses where they ate dust and dust spewed
from their dust-pummeled bodies. Families fled
the plains in droves while those who stayed wept
tears that turned to mud beneath the wet flour
sacks wrapped around their faces, and breathing
became the hardest work of all. Still, dust black
as soot rose from the barren fields like swarms
of bees and locusts. And there was no surcease
of suffering until the day it rained when the land
cupped its dust-covered hands, and drank.

THE MAN WHO CUTS HIS GRASS WITH NAIL SCISSORS

On a corner lot in Buena Vista, lives
a man who cuts his grass
with nail scissors.

He is very thin, and can curl his body
into many shapes, like the hands
of a shadow puppeteer—

or a boy used to settling
into lockers where he's been shoved,
waiting hours

to be rescued. His gaze never veers
to passing cars, nor do greetings
from his neighbors

get an answer. Lopping off the heads
of every clover, squaring the tips
of every blade takes

time, but he clips until the lawn is level—
the way that *playing fields*
have never been, or ever will be.

TV DINNER

Home from school with a sore throat, I didn't want soup.
TV dinners were what I begged my mother for—the kind
that came with cornbread dressing nestled beneath white
slabs of turkey, brown gravy sloshed on top as if a hair-
netted, poker-faced lunch lady slung it there, shouting *next!*
And then there was the cranberry sauce with its gelatinous
quiver, like red *Jello* only darker, thicker, with just a hint
of sour—mashed potatoes that tasted more like hot, buttered
cardboard. Last came the square of yellow cake so small
I could eat it in three bites, savoring that brief sweetness
on my tongue, though I could hardly swallow. Best of all
was the sectioned plate and the shiny tin it was made
from—how my spoon slid across its smooth, silver bottom
before it hit a wall between one food and another, neatly
separated, organized to perfection. I had learned, already,
how messy life can be, that some people won't like you
no matter what you do, that even grown-ups can be cruel.
But lying on the couch in our living room watching cartoons
on a week day, pillows plumped against my back, TV
dinner on a tray, and my mother hovering close by, feeling
my forehead for fever—it felt as if the jumbled hours of days
when I was well were just a dream, that this ordered world
where I was safe and loved, was the only one that counted.

AMSALE SALON

Madison Avenue, New York

Crafted from your dreams, the perfect
wedding gown waits suspended above a simple
wooden floor like a dancer's

costume lifted into the air without her. Bride
after bride will slide her soft fingers
across the silk,

satin, organza and tulle—admire the sculpted
floral embellishments, crystal
beaded belts and cascading

ruffle backs. But only your heart beating
beneath its hand-draped bodice, its sweetheart
neckline, can bring the dress

to life. This cloud-like confection is a vase
without a flower until you, the woman for whom
your gown was made, finds it.

IRISES

for Stephen White

By the stone wall on top
of which my mother balanced as a child,

grow the purple irises
my grandmother planted, still blooming.

The house is there, as well, but the paint
is peeling, the front porch

collapsing. The man inside carries
a baseball bat,

peers at us through the bulging screen
door like we've come to rob

the place, though we are not the trouble
he's been waiting for—just a family

searching for the past, saddened
by what we see. That's when Stephen

spies the irises. Then the once familiar
house, frightening in its strangeness,

takes on a kindlier air,
as if the woman kneeling by the walk

decades before, digging up the rich, red
dirt, pushing bulbs into holes

she made in the ground, is still there—
and we are all welcome.

BIRD

The day he left, his mother claimed she couldn't
afford to feed him. *You're a man now*, she said,
her face hard as sidewalks after the cement sets.
He packed what little he owned in a paper sack
to the sound of his sisters crying, his eight-
year-old brother screaming *don't go, don't go,*
until their mother smacked him in the mouth
and he went silent. For weeks the boy trudged
up and down the city streets, growing thinner
and dirtier—the veins in his temples throbbing
like neon signs against a backdrop of skin so fine,
you could put your finger through it—or so it
seemed to people passing by, before turning
away fast. So when a savior appeared, a man
who looked like someone's father, offering him
food and drink, clothing and shelter, the boy's
gratitude was such that he didn't mind at first,
doing anything to please him. But the men kept
coming, one after the other, using him like an old
rag they tossed away when they were done. So he
opened a window in the locked room ten stories
above the pavement, but there was no standing on
the ledge, no gathering crowds or sirens wailing—
just a swift leap into the warm night air that felt
like bathwater back in the days his mother loved
him, though people who saw him jump swore they
thought this boy, fifteen tomorrow, was just a bird.

Runners

A team of runners, shorts loose as time on their lanky
frames, crosses the road in single file, arms
and legs pumping. Slicker than eels

and soaked with sweat, their bodies buck the current
that carries them toward the old man

on the corner, relying on his cane to keep him upright—
zoom past him and every spent commuter waiting

for the light to change—as if a glorious future beckons
beyond the stippled trees, the next steep hill,
and all they have to do is catch it.

VÄSTERÅS, SWEDEN

Though Gun and Gösta are gone, the seasons
come and go, and summer is winding down
around their country cabin, close to Motts' farm.
Light that lingers through the night is fading
lately, in length and luster. Soon, darkness
will spread its thick cloak in mid-afternoon,
over fields missing the hay that has long
since been harvested—giant rolls that looked
from the air, like great beasts felled by sleep.
But until the North wind blows its frozen breath
across this light-addled, sun-drunk land, Motts'
enormous cows—their swollen udders swinging
beneath their sleek, golden bodies—will graze
on soft, gilded grass. And the calm waters
of Lake Mälaren will lap its reedy shores until
the surface turns to ice and can move no more.
Then perhaps, you'll hear an echo from winters
past—the sound of Gösta's ax, chopping wood
for the fire—or see the glow from lit lamps
spilling across the snow-covered yard when Gun,
her voice warm as soup simmering on the stove,
opens the door and calls to her husband—who
gathers all the wood he can carry, and hurries in.

CRUSH

I am crazy-mad in love with a smooth-talking,
long-haired boy, who smells like the devil
on a date. Too bad my mother would kill me
if I so much as spoke his name, and he is not

allowed on our property, according to my daddy,
a man with a double-barrel shotgun and a mean

disposition. But when that boy watches me
cross the schoolyard, his eyes feel like black

marbles rolling all over my skin, making me
fidgety as Mama's prize pullet when that old
rooster of ours jumps on a fence and crows.

One minute I want to run and hide; the next
I'd like to yank him into the ryegrass over

that hill yonder and do what I keep hearing
the eighth grade girls go on about—

the same girls he's usually with when he's
staring at me. I can't grow up fast enough,
is all I can say, and from the look on that boy's
face when I walk by, he can't wait, either.

Bertram Baumgartner, Town Grocer

I swannee, Bertram, said his wife of fifteen years,
you have got to stop giving away our inventory! He hung
his head low, knowing she was right, as usual. But he
wouldn't stop extending credit to people who really needed

it, particularly his third and fourth cousins twice removed—
they were family, after all—and a few hardworking
folks from the *Happy Camper Trailer Park,* whose children,

bless their hearts, were cute as ten buckets of buttons
with their slow smiles and shy ways, so grateful for one piece
of hard candy. He couldn't help but think of his son, Bertram,
Jr., who had everything a boy could ask for

and still wanted more. He stopped listening when his wife
reached the part about how they were all headed straight
for the poorhouse since there was no such thing as a poorhouse
these days and besides, they had plenty of money—

enough to last long after they were gone. He shuddered
to think what Bertram, Jr. would do with his inheritance—
probably spend every dime on himself, making Bertram, Sr.

wish for the hundredth time that his own first grade teacher,
Miss Annie Maude Montgomery, had been his boy's teacher,
too, instead of that woman from Charlotte who never seemed

to understand that this was a small town with small town ways.
As far as he was concerned, teaching kids to do unto others

was way more important than any subject, including math,
which Bertram, Jr., come to think of it, always passed with flying
colors—probably because he thought it would help him
count his father's hard-earned cash.

Fox

Bald Head Island, NC

Midday, midsummer, the fox
slinks into the road, leaving the dark weald
trembling in his wake. His pupils

are dilated; limbs slow to obey
as he squats, squirting a thin stream of hot
contagion that splatters across

the pavement. Like a drunk who tries
and fails to hit the urinal, he lurches away
from the mess he's made,

then moves toward us, his gaze black
as charred wood—his wild, rabid body red
as the flames that burned it.

SLAVE CEMETERY

Even as children, we sensed the slave cemetery
called for silence. We had no problem shouting
in the graveyard near our grandmother's house.
There, every plot was like a well-kept lawn—
the grass green and tender, the ground flat above
the graves as if there were no bodies buried beneath
the packed-down soil and strips of carefully laid
sod. Families filled brass urns with silk flowers—
jaunty bouquets dyed to match the season. Such
brilliant colors gave each site an air of celebration,
as if death were just a party we would all one day
attend—the markers like place cards on a fancy
dinner table. But in the slave cemetery, we couldn't
tell whose names were carved into the moss-covered
stones, cracked or crumbling. Some graves were
sunken as toothless faces. Others bore mounds
that looked freshly made, as if the dead could burst
free any moment, from dirt so loosely tamped on top
of their bones. And there was no grass or flowers,
only creeping vegetation that smelled of damp
and rot, bushes with thorns and trees with roots
so fat and twisted, they looked like anacondas
sleeping in the underbrush. In the slave cemetery,
death was tied forever to loss and sorrow, and we
were sorry. So we tiptoed around the tombs, quiet
as clouds. People buried here, deserve their rest.

IV

TICKLE PINK INN

Glistening like the pink pulp of organic grapefruit
gracing the porcelain plates of movie stars,
another special offer from the Tickle Pink Inn
sits in my Inbox. This 35-room luxury hotel nestled

against the rocky cliffs of Carmel, California,
promises ocean views, cozy European bedding,

and homemade breakfast pastries served alongside
your personal copy of the morning newspaper.

Every photograph from any angle could be a slice
of heaven carved out and hand-delivered to lucky
winners who come from all over the country

to curl in front of wood-burning fireplaces and sip
complimentary glasses of champagne

with husbands, wives, lovers, or friends. If only we
could all go there, just once—to lay our burdens

down and bask in the sun's lemony glow on balconies
overlooking the light-dappled waves, so tickled pink
we forget whatever pain life has bestowed upon us
and fall in love again, with the world.

NEIGHBOR BOY

Close but not touching,
the neighbor boy

and his new girlfriend
stroll around the block

at least a dozen times,
delighting the dogs

that bark, the children
who wave at them,

and middle-aged
women, whose memory

of the first boy we
wished on stars to keep,

is one of the few things
we haven't yet lost.

HALL TREE

Papa knew the shape a man's body
takes when he comes home from work,
weary—how Granny's back bowed
over a butter churn, bent to lift a child
or slip a pair of well-worn shoes from
her tired feet. So after he cut wood
for the hall tree, he soaked it in water
to make it curve the way a spine
curves, from top to base, four long
pieces of timber facing each other,
like family around a table. And every
evening he'd hang his hand-woven
Panama hat on one of its cast iron
hooks that to this day holds the same
hat in the corner of my kitchen. You'd
think he just walked through the door
and hung it there himself—that any
minute now, his wife will join him
and they'll sit together on my front
porch—Granny's face puckered
like an old lemon turning in on
itself, the ribbons on her bonnet tied
tight around her snuff-stained chin,
and Papa, grinning and waving
at people passing by, sawdust falling
from his arm like flakes of snow.

ANGELS OF DEATH

Identical twins, the *Angels of Death* dressed
alike—had done so from the time of fig

leaves. They owned a rent-controlled
apartment in Manhattan, but were seldom

in residence, what with all the dead to gather.
They divided the work in half, although

the oldest (or so he claimed) took the hard
cases. *I have the stomach for it,* he said.

You, dear brother, do not. So the murders
belonged to him as well as suicides—

and soldiers killed in war. They were bloated,
beaten, shot and mutilated, their bodies

left behind like spent cartridges—while his
brother took the children, the sick and elderly—

their souls lighter than parchment paper,
easy to peel away. And who can truly say

which angel is more terrible—the one striding
across a battlefield, covered in human blood,

or his twin, tip-toeing into bedrooms, stealing
sleeping babies from their mothers' arms?

TAMMY LYNN MOFFITT

Tammy Lynn was a beautiful baby—blue-eyed
and blonde-headed. Her ringlets bobbed like corks
in a stream every time she hopped,
skipped and jumped down the lane past the shanty-house
where she lived with her parents and three rowdy

brothers. Some said Tammy took to the streets
to get away from her drunken daddy, but mostly it

was a desperate desire to be loved
that drove her into the arms of strangers.
It seemed like there wasn't enough love
in the whole world to fill Tammy Lynn's well of need.

Finally, she gave up on love altogether and started
charging cash-money for men to sample charms
she kept until her late thirties,

when her face seemed to wither and cave in like a rotting
mushroom. She took to wearing sunglasses
and black-veiled hats like some movie star who didn't want
to be recognized, only everybody knew exactly

who and what she was. Most women kept a good bit
of room between them and her; and their husbands, well,

there was still something about Tammy Lynn Moffitt
that sent an electrical current through their veins
despite the fact that she covered herself with widow's weeds—
as if anybody would ever be foolish enough to marry
Tammy Lynn—although eventually,
somebody did.

TRASH MAN

Back in the days when everything seemed miraculous
and permanent, people kept metal garbage cans
in their backyards instead of the plastic ones we wheel
every Wednesday now to the curb. So when the trash
truck came squealing into the neighborhood, it stopped
on our street and out popped two or three barrel-toting
trash men wearing thick gloves and filthy jumpsuits.
They'd spin their dirty drums with the same motion
our father used when waxing his car, only ten times
faster, making a gravelly sound you couldn't mistake
for anything else. Depending on how early it was,
we pressed our noses against the kitchen window or quit
playing ball long enough to watch them toss those gray,
saucer-shaped lids on the ground, lift the cans and dump
a week's worth of garbage into the barrels. We wondered
how they stood the stench or brought themselves to touch
those nasty bins around which we kept such a wide berth.
But these guys whistled while they worked and waved
at us kids idle in our yards and houses—smiled like men
rolling the moon from one side of the sky to the other
instead of all the stuff that people didn't need or want—
the detritus of so many lives, laid bare.

ANTS

The sidewalk
scratchy
on my belly
where my t-shirt
rode up,
I studied
a colony
of ants
scurrying
in and out
of a tiny
crack in
the pavement.
Fascinated,
my eight-year-old
self wondered
what it must
be like to navigate
that narrow
passage down
a dark
hole, blind,
then up
again,
your dull,
brown body
bearing
a single
grain of sand,
(twenty times
your weight),
beneath
the watchful
gaze of giants.

Working Tobacco

At 5 a.m. for three solid months the summer
my father, Tom, turned fourteen, Bobby Kimel and his step-dad
would swing by my grandparents' house on Druid Hill Drive
and pick him up from the curb. I can see my father now, short,
scrawny, a constellation of freckles flecking his nose
and cheeks, buck teeth and black hair—wide awake and eager
to make some spending money.

Dropped off at a dairy farm in Kernersville
where tobacco was the cash crop, the boys ate breakfast,
then started suckering—a filthy, backbreaking job
that meant walking up and down the rows, removing tender
sprouts at every junction of leaf and stalk, the black, sticky tobacco
gum crawling up their arms and ruining their clothes,
the humid air hot as Satan's belt buckle.

While they were at it, they checked each plant for worms,
fat as fingers, then pinched off their heads and tossed their bodies
to the ground. When priming time rolled around, they'd pull
the bottom three leaves from every stalk and load them into tobacco
sleds hitched to the horse or mule they weren't supposed to ride
but did sometimes, when nobody was looking.
Come noon, the owner served

Tom and Bobby sandwiches from his general store,
and milk from his own dairy cows. You've never tasted milk
like that, my father says—chilled with lumps of cream floating
in the foam and we drank every drop, he tells me, before heading back
to the blistering fields where they'd work all the hours
before dark, getting paid at the end of the day
like full-grown men.

BATTERED

She stands in the hallway, holding a dog by the collar.
Her hair is wispy and thin, her teeth crooked. The dog
growls deep in its barreled chest; her frown lines
lengthen. She knows not to answer the door. Her husband
wouldn't like it. But nothing she does is right, so what
does it matter? Bruises bloom and fade. Days bleed
into weeks. She has no friends, no family—only a dog
that hates everyone, and photographs she keeps in a box
beneath the bed. There are snapshots of her parents, arms
looped around each other, herself as a child—serious,
brooding, perhaps sensing already, the life that she will live.
Now there is a stranger on the stoop, a man who might do
anything. She pictures angels lifting her soul to heaven,
wonders if they sing to you on the way up. She can
almost hear them as the door opens, feel the brush
of wings when she lets him in.

DRIVE-BY

Pacing the sidewalk, a woman in dark,
dusty clothes—hair tangled in oily clumps
beside her bloated cheeks—carries a cardboard

sign that says, *help me*, scribbled in red
crayon. There is no explanation like *homeless*

veteran or *single mother out of work*,
just *help me*, something most of us can relate
to as we sit in our heated cars on a crisp fall

morning, bellies full of lattes or bacon biscuits,
knowing we are inches from losing everything—

our jobs, our homes, our minds. So we look
away when we pass by, as if her face is the one
stone that could shatter our lives, like glass.

AFTER THE FUNERAL

Mourners came and went all day,
tossing casseroles and apple pies
into the greedy maw of grief, though
it was never satisfied. Their faces,
bleached by sorrow, belonged to people
we loved, neighbors we knew and even
strangers—friends of friends who came
to pay their respects. But my mother
wanted no part of it. She was locked
in the bedroom, laboring hard. It is
work when you are middle-aged, giving
birth to the same boy you brought home
twenty years before. But it is necessary.
Otherwise, how will you believe it? They
say you had a son, but you can't find him.
His clothes are in the closet; his shoes
on the stairs. There are pictures of him
everywhere, but the boy, himself, is gone.
So she is busy, pushing her child into
the world, watching him walk, then run,
then vanish as if he were never born.
Yet, he was. The pain proves it.

DANCE NIGHT, BLOOMINGTON

On the corner of Sixth and Walnut, in a room above the Subway
Shop, is a dance studio with windows so wide and well-lit,
they look like movie screens. And if you stop to catch your breath
while walking, or pause to feed more change into a parking meter,
look up. Perhaps you'll catch a class in progress,
witness for yourself the grace
and style of an old man, sway-backed and slow, salsa dancing
with his partner. Her hair is silver, gathered at the neck by a rhinestone
clip—and she is smiling. They are gliding across a floor
that none of us can see, beneath a ceiling high enough that stars,
dangling from the night sky, might sometimes touch
the roof above it with their sparkly feet. And as different dancers
salsa in and out of view, you can't stop watching.
You long, in fact, to find a partner among the strangers hurrying
by you, to join hands and feel whatever it is that makes these couples'
faces radiant, their bodies circle around a room built to let light
in and to shine light out—illuminating the town
and all its people like the sun and moon might do together,
if only they could dance.

V

WOMAN ON THE DOCK

Early morning, the sun looks like the last butter cookie
on a blue plate of sky. Gulls are swarming
over the channel the way bees will, around an empty
Coke can that still smells of sugar. Somewhere in the water,
a fish is swimming through silt and seaweed, a ray or two of light
flickering on its gills like flames. In five minutes it will find my bait,
maybe ten. I am optimistic. And when it bites, the line
will feel like one long nerve connecting the fish's body
to mine as if I've already scaled, gutted,
cooked and swallowed it—making it as much a part
of what I am as my arms, my hands. Then the ocean will live
inside of me, the salt of it, the cool,
the way it kisses the coastline some days and pounds it like a fist
on others. I can be a wave, a tide. I can wait for a fish
as long as it takes to catch it.

VULTURE

Surrounded by the short stubble of stalks cut
close to the ground, a turkey vulture
stands in an Indiana

cornfield, wings spread. It is motionless—
quiet as the carrion it consumes—
its pinions casting

a six-foot shadow on the chill earth that serves
most often, as its dinner plate.
But there is no rush on cold winter

mornings, to soar in circles searching
for what is dead or dying.
Buzzards prefer to warm their bones and dry

their feathers first. And though it feeds
on death, the vulture—alive in this moment
as a buck in the woods,

seconds before the shot—resembles
not so much a bird of prey, but a black-clad
mourner

who has paused outside the church to watch
the sun come up: arms open wide,
embracing the world while he still can.

LIGHTS OUT, CHARLIE

For my grandfather, John H. Kirby, Sr.,
Air Raid Warden, 1942

Steel helmet on his head, flashlight in hand,
you could tell the air raid warden was ready to go
as soon as the siren sounded. It wasn't where he
wanted to be, but the Navy turned him down flat
and a man had to do something for the war effort,
didn't he? So he'd swiftly circle the block, make
sure the curtains in every house were drawn,
the lights switched off—that nobody was outside,
roaming the streets. After all, it might not always
be a drill. The bombers could come and if they
did, his brother would show them the way.
Time and time again he'd say, *Lights out, Charlie,*
and Charlie would oblige for as long as it took
the air raid warden to step away from the porch.
Well, he couldn't report his own flesh and blood,
though you'd think his brother would do what he
was told for his own good and everybody else's.
Charlie never believed the enemy would get
anywhere near North Carolina and they hadn't
yet, but who could say for certain? *I'd rather die*
than sit in the dark, said the cheap son-of-a-gun,
who owned a cinderblock store full of candy and pop
he never once let his nieces and nephews have for free.
He felt bad that Charlie's house was just past the city
line, which meant no water, no indoor plumbing.
But by God, he had electric lights in there and nights
like this when the siren was blaring out a warning,
the warden felt like bashing every lit bulb to bits
with a baseball bat. And then a feeling would come
over him that brought tears to his eyes, imagining
his big brother sitting in his own house sweating,
terrified, unable to see his hand in front of his face
and, well, he'd just walk on, praying the enemy never
showed up—wishing he were on a battleship far
out to sea, the moon the only light for miles and miles.

ORCHID

Psychological freedom, a firm sense
of self-esteem, is the most powerful weapon
against the long night of physical slavery.
—Martin Luther King, Jr.

Nights, I am a moth orchid
with petals soft as a mother's kiss,
white as wedding veils.

Nothing touches me but moonlight—
and through an open window,
rain. Days, a patch

of sky blue enough to fool a fish
into thinking I am water—and angels
fly right through me, hurrying

toward the sound of prayer.
I can be anything but the poor girl
trapped inside this helpless

body. She belongs to everyone
who pays, forced to bear the weight
of monsters in the shape of men.

NANNIE WHITE

Nannie White cradled Clyde Willis
in her lap, crooned a song he was partial
to hearing, come bedtime. They tried to take him
from her, claiming it wasn't decent
to keep a corpse aboveground so long,
but she held on tight.

What a good boy he is—
always minding his mama, never pitching
a fit to get his own way. And Lord knows,
he was the prettiest baby she ever saw—
eyes bluer than birdsfoot violets, cheeks red
as holly berries.

She could hear them milling around
on the front porch. *She's plum out of her mind*
with grief. Can't you do something with her, Sam?
They ought to know better than to ask him.
He's a smooth talker,
my Samuel,

but you can't talk a woman's child
out of her arms. *I won't give in to it,* she said,
pain sharp as a stick poking her heart.
If I do, I'll crumble like an old wasp nest,
leaving Clyde Willis
to wake up, alone.

OLD MAN ON A GLIDER

He used to sit on a glider somebody
drug close to the road, wearing
blue jean coveralls and a beat-up

straw hat, cocked sideways. He
waved at every car careening around
the curve as if they were neighbors

come to call, arms laden with chicken
casserole and blueberry cobbler—
fishing poles tossed in the trunk,

just in case. We might set up a game
of checkers, pitch horseshoes in
the backyard. But we kept going

and he kept waving until the day
he didn't—that old glider back on
the front porch, empty as a promise.

BLACKIE AND BROWNIE

Sometimes we were a couple of cowpokes
cantering through a quiet town. The saloon
was open for business, but it was too early
in the morning for gunfights or shootouts—
nobody placing bets or brawling over bar girls
sleeping upstairs, their ruby dresses and white
lace petticoats slung across the backs of chairs.
We'd almost fall asleep ourselves, listening
to the rhythmic clip-clop of our horses' hooves—
though the occasional grunt of a ranch hand
hoisting bags of feed into a wagon and the hourly
peal of church bells kept us from sliding off
our mounts into the dust. Other times, we tore
through the *Lone Prairie* in constant mortal
danger from sidewinders and rattlesnakes, bandits
and braves—the next town so far in the distance
we knew we'd never make it there before breakfast.
So when our mother called our names, we'd prop
those trusty steeds, Blackie and Brownie, in the
corner of the kitchen—their vinyl heads beaded
with sweat, stick bodies worn to a splinter from
all the hours my brother and I spent together,
riding tall in the saddle.

PHOTOGRAPH

by Jun Itoi, from Cantos Familia

In the foreground, flowers bloom unfocused—
glow like gaslight against the dark grass,
the silent water. They seem attached

to nothing, yet they hover inches above
the earth like souls released from heavy bodies,
reluctant to move on. Who can blame

them? The band of sky, captured by
the camera's click, is lapis-blue—the billowing
clouds, white as sheets clipped

to a clothesline. And just outside the frame,
a mother calls her child's name.
He is seconds away from answering.

PINK DUMPSTERS

Barreling down the highway on the back of a big rig,
seven brand-new, Pepto-Bismol-pink dumpsters
are headed for who knows where. Plastic lids flapping
in the wind, they seem to be having lively conversations,
like ladies standing in long checkout lines
do sometimes, when they get bored. Or maybe
they're old friends, having met at the dumpster factory,
and are busy saying good-bye. Doubtless there are seven
pink dumpster buyers waiting for delivery in different
parts of the country—or at least, separate locations on the same
property—maybe a luxury hotel in the Keys, taking their tropical
attire into account. Anyway, they seem to be excited,
perhaps not yet aware of what people do with dumpsters—
that soon their bright, shiny interiors, slick and pink
as a cat's mouth, will be smeared with substances best
left unmentioned. They're just seven garrulous
girls in matching outfits, more interested
in each other than their destination.

Night Watchman

Our father, wearing cotton pajama bottoms
and a white t-shirt—the thin, comfortable kind
with a few holes here and there, for ventilation—

made the rounds at night, locking all the doors,
turning out the lights. We could hear him

from our beds upstairs if we were still awake,
picture his familiar face striped with shadows
from trees next to the windows as the moon

rose high in the sky, and the street lamp burned
bright on the corner. It was he and he alone

who stood between whatever it was that lurked
in the dark woods, the deserted roads—

and his family. But since it was our father
watching over us like a sentry, we slept secure,
certain he would keep us safe from harm.

HIGH COUNTRY WINTER

Drifts of hard-packed snow press against
the house and a cold wind howls like shipwrecked
ghosts, locked between the ridges of these ancient
mountains. An old hound dog warms
his haunches by the fire; his master nods

in his chair by the hearth. Wrapped in heavy,
woolen blankets, a hunter's cap pulled low

on his brow, he dreams of walking
through a meadow, thick with hydrangea and goat's
beard, bee balm and trillium. His wife, Mary,
beckons—her eyes morning-glory-blue, her hands
soft and white as asters blooming by the gate.

Ice Cream Truck

From blocks away we heard the mechanical
music the ice cream truck chimed all over
the neighborhood, calling to kids like the Pied

Piper as we darted into our houses begging
our parents for change to buy Nutty Buddies

and banana popsicles, orange pushups
and ice cream sandwiches. Once the truck

stopped on our street, we swooped like seagulls
around the open window so the ice cream man
could take our money and hand out whatever

treats we asked for, which were always better
than we remembered from the last time his boxy,

hand-painted truck rolled around—the cold,
creamy confections freezing our tongues and

sliding down our parched throats as fast as we
could eat them—the taste of summer lingering
just long enough to make us wish for more.

At the Wafflehouse

Sunday mornings at the Waffle House are a sight to see,
what with pancakes flying around the room like Frisbees,
the floor so sticky with syrup, people get stuck sometimes,
so every waitress keeps a butter knife in her pocket

to pry the patrons loose. And if it's eggs you're looking
for, you've come to the right place. They've got omelets,
of course, and anything edible you want to put in one, if they
can find it in the freezer. Or you can have your eggs boiled,

poached, sunny-side-up, over-easy, in-a-nest or scrambled.
Some eggs, however, defy description, which is when
a customer says something like, *Don't make my egg too
hard. Leave it kindly runny, but not too runny, or the dad-*

blame thing might get away from me! which always puts
the cook in a fine mood. But when it comes to the Waffle
House specialty, the human mind can hardly wrap itself
around so many mouth-watering choices. To name a few,

there's Belgian waffles or regular; buckwheat or buttermilk;
plain, banana, blueberry, raspberry, strawberry, boysenberry,
chocolate chip and pumpkin; with powdered sugar or without;
and you can add whipped cream if you're feeling frisky.

If you want meat on the side, pork is generally the way to go,
but turkey's popular, too, particularly if your cholesterol number
would make a better bowling score. As for beverages, there
are buckets of milk; orange, tomato and grapefruit juice;

and so much coffee, just sniffing the air will make your heart
beat like a piston, prompting most people to eat their breakfast
pronto, making way for the next group before you can say
hash browns. And speaking of groups, there are all sorts

of folks who frequent the Waffle House on Sunday mornings.
First of all, you'll find kids of every shape, size, age,
and temperament, including the blessedly well-behaved
and plum-out-of-control, which means they're screaming,

fighting, spraying their parents with tomato ketchup and making
any person within earshot, which is usually the whole building,
as miserable as possible. And the adults come in variety
packs, too, including married couples who barely say

two words to each other; teenagers who can't stop talking
long enough to eat; bikers covered in tattoos and so many
metal piercings they jingle when they walk; suntanned
retirees; golfers who stopped by on their way to teeing off;

and people so hung over from Saturday night, they sit at the
counter, where they feel most comfortable anyway, ordering
nothing but gallons of black coffee. And the waitresses are
mostly good-hearted souls unless you forget to mind your

manners, in which case it's not their fault if your plate slips
from the tray and lands in your lap. Come lunchtime, however,
the crowd changes over to church-goers and late-risers, gradually
thinning out to nothing around mid-afternoon, when every

waitress, cook, and dishwasher's dogs are barking up a storm
and every customer who's eaten at the Waffle House is either at
home in a carb-induced coma, or bouncing off the walls someplace—
so full of sugar and caffeine, they might never sit down again.

BLACKBIRD

Hands in the kitchen sink,
a woman watches a red-winged
blackbird rise from a fence.

It flies farther and farther away,
over the distant cornfields,
the silos, barns

and houses—then disappears
like dishwater down a drain,
leaving the sky clean.

VI

THE DIRT ROAD

Circling the dirt road, feet bare,
we compared notes about the boys we thought were cute,
though we were far too young and bony yet
for them to notice. Sixteen, at least,
they cruised the same few blocks, suntanned arms dangling
from the driver's side of their daddies' Chevrolet Impalas
and Chrysler LeBarons like the tails of big cats
flicking in the grass as they watch their prey—
while the girls they wanted pretended

not to see them. These girls swanned around
the neighborhood swinging their hips like church bells,
curls bouncing on shoulders soft as ripe peaches, lipstick red
as home-grown tomatoes on mouths that knew how to kiss,
or so we believed—though they would never
tell us, even if we had the nerve

to ask. In those days, the tiny nubbins of our breasts
seemed like seeds that would never sprout,
and we couldn't keep our hair combed
more than five minutes before the strands turned to strings.
But we ached for something when we saw those boys
that neither of us could name. So we went walking, waved
at the old couple sitting on their front porch the way
they always did of a summer evening
when it was cooler outside than inside the house.

STEVIE SANTOS

Stevie Santos wore his sister's slingbacks
to class, her false eyelashes. Silk shirts clung,
half-buttoned,

to his milk-white chest. Kids stared
and snickered, but Stevie's eyes faced forward,
like a soldier. With bombs of ridicule

exploding so close they might have blown him
to pieces, he marched down the pea-green
hallways of his father's alma mater,

painted toenails glittering. His step never
faltered—as if he saw clear through their jeering
faces to a tropical rainforest,

where birds with jeweled feathers called to one
another from the emerald trees—and nothing
on the ground could touch them.

TEXAS HOLD'EM

As light settles soft as the gloaming
on their bowed heads, players glance
at the cards they were dealt and place
their bets. Huddled over half-moon poker
tables, they sit elbow-to-elbow, smoking
cigarettes, nursing free drinks or tossing
them back one after the other, until the cards
blur in their hands and luck is just a cruel
coquette, leading them further and further
into debt. Still, it's cozy here, playing
Texas Hold'em with friends they don't know
and a dealer who looks sad when he rakes
their chips away, happy when he doles out
more—who says *Good Luck* before every
hand is played, as if he means it. And the pit
bosses in their coats and ties, crisp dress shirts
and shiny shoes, seem capable of handling
any crisis, of keeping it all under control
as they stroll from table to table, their faces
impassive, almost benevolent, as if they,
too, are rooting for the players. But it's the
occasional four-of-a-kind or full house that
keeps hope alive, though people seldom quit
when they're ahead. They burn through hundred
dollar bills like kindling, until they have no
choice but to give up their warm seats to other
wannabe millionaires waiting their turn to win
big, then lose everything they've got, like you.

AGNES

My mother's black baby doll wore a gingham
dress. Her head was covered in pigtails, her brown

feet bare. Back then, you could hardly find
such a thing among the millions

of lily-white dolls with blonde hair and blue eyes,
babies that said, "Mama!" when you turned them

over. But the black doll was silent, called for nobody—
was given to her by Agnes, who did the washing

up, the ironing—took care of her while her parents
were at work. If my mother had been a doll,

she would have cried "Agnes!" when you turned
her over, since Agnes was the one who answered—

the woman who dried her tears,
whose arms were like a cradle, rocking.

VINCENZOS

The back door opened and a rectangle of light
became a gold carpet on the parking lot pavement
as the building sighed the way we all do after a good
meal, scenting the air with fresh garlic, oregano,
and basil. We could see from our car, the people
inside, bustling—a man tossing pizza dough into the air
and catching it with his fist, another ladling minestrone
and pasta fazool into heavy soup bowls for the pretty
waitress who zoomed in and zoomed out, ponytail
bouncing to the beat of a busboy's tenor, the clatter
of pots and pans, the rhythmic rumble of busy
feet zig-zagging across the tiled floor. And as we
sat there in the dark, watching, we wanted to bypass
the front entrance, altogether—the neon sign, the hostess
at her station—and slip instead, into the warm kitchen
with its hustle and hurry, its buttery glow. We pictured
ourselves sitting at the stainless steel prep table, talking,
laughing, even pitching in if they could find some use
for a long-married, middle-aged couple with no one left
at home to feed, but ourselves. And then the door closed,
the light disappeared, and we felt as bereft as people
in a theater when a film that moved us all to tears, ends.

Rose

Her hair sparse and white as snow dusting a sidewalk,
Rose reclines in the chemo room, her body hidden

beneath a bee-patterned blanket. She struggles to stay
awake as clear fluid drips, slow and steady, into her vein.

Her eyelids open and close, flutter like moths over lapis
pools of water. At times like this, the tubing that tethers

her to this world seems more fragile than the glass stem
of a champagne flute—as if anything might break it—

a child's breath, a slight breeze, the barely perceptible
stir of another soul freed today from suffering.

MAKING CORNBREAD

"There's more to it than you think," the old woman
said, sitting on the steps of a house with a roof
that sagged in the center, like a worn-out mattress.
"Two cups of Tenda-Bake self-rising corn meal
is best, but don't get the yellow; get the white. One
and a fourth cups of milk ought to be about right;
one egg you need to beat a little bit before you add
it to the batter; and a fourth of a cup of oil. Oh, you
can use any kind of vegetable oil and even shortening,
if you want to. I use Wesson, but it's up to you.
Have you got all that?" she said, peering over the rims
of her glasses, her hair sticking up like a hen's comb
in the middle of her head. She never worried about
what people thought of her looks, anyway, which she
claims to have lost when a tornado took her barn in '89.
"Aged me ten years in a split second," she said, "and
I ain't cared since then, to waste my time with mirrors."
She went on to say, "You mix all them ingredients,
but don't stir too much or your batter won't rise.
And you've got to have the right skillet. If you don't
use a cast-iron skillet, you might as well forget the whole
thing. And heat it in the oven first, before you pour
the batter in. Be careful, though. You can get a right
smart burn if you don't watch out. Keep them oven
mitts handy!" she said, cackling like a witch flying
across the moon. "You set the heat at 400 degrees,
by the way, and don't open the oven door until your
cornbread's been cooking at least 25 minutes if you
don't want it coming out flat as griddle-cakes." Dabbing
her nose with a wadded-up Kleenex, she leaned in close
and said, "Don't forget, when you're making cornbread

or anything else, to say a prayer. It don't have to be
much, but pray loud enough so the Lord can hear you
talking. He gets mighty lonesome up there when folks
forget to say hello. Go ahead and laugh, but mark
my words, there's nothing like prayed-over cornbread.
It rises like souls on their way to heaven, and melts
in your mouth like butter, which, of course, you ought
to slather on top once you put a piece on your plate.
Oh, and if you like your cornbread sweet, add a pinch
of sugar to the batter, which never hurt anybody as far as
I can tell, and some people's dispositions are improved by it."

ZORA-MAY PETTIGREW

Despite being the town's wealthiest citizen, Zora-May
Pettigrew wore second-hand clothes she bought
at the consignment shop. She ate dinner every night
by candlelight, but she was no romantic—

far from it. In fact, she swore off men back in '93
after one date with that loud-mouthed mayor

Roscoe Poteet, who bored her silly with his continuous
gum-flapping soliloquies and patting himself on the back
for going out with a black woman as if he deserved
an award for it. Nobody cared

about that sort of thing, anymore—nobody she wanted
to know, anyway. The more he talked, the more

she thought about that croquet mallet she hid under
the couch in case a cat burglar broke in. Lord knows,
she was not a violent woman by nature, but an hour or two
of Roscoe Poteet's pontificating

would provoke a saint. Truth be known,
other than her tendency to hold onto a dollar bill for at least
five minutes before handing it over, Zora-May Pettigrew

was an old softie. She kept the children's section
at the public library stocked with crisp new books, and every
year she threw a birthday party

for Tammy Lynn Moffitt Wainwright and her husband,
the Honorable Judge Lester Wainwright. Most of the town's
female population wouldn't be caught dead in the same

room with Tammy, married or not, and most of the men
were either former clients or admirers, so despite their regard
for the Judge—and envy, if truth be known,

they couldn't bring themselves to attend. So it was just
the three of them, which meant there was plenty
of good cheer, pink lemonade squares and sweet tea
with fresh mint, to go around.

BEE KEEPER

When morning broke across his back
and sunlight yellow as yolks woke
the sleeping bees because they do sleep,
contrary to rumor—mostly in the hive

but sometimes resting on a flower—
Papa must have felt, listening to them
hum, that he would live forever.

So much life buzzing around his head
and landing on his shoulders as he went

about his work—picturing all the while
a pat of butter fresh from the churn,
melting inside a homemade, honey-

sopped biscuit. But the scent of sugar
is all that pierced the netting swathed
around his face, and he never wore gloves.
Only the thought of change, ever stung him.

PALMIST

Perhaps roadside palmists take a vow of poverty.
Nothing else explains, when they know all, the tattered
curtains, the tacky neon signs in dirt-streaked windows
that flicker on and off when trucks roar by, as if these splayed
fingers, those disembodied digits, are waving us in through
the flimsy front doors, the rooms behind beaded curtains
that part like water. You seldom find palmists puttering
around their yards, trimming rose bushes, mulching,
making the mysterious seem ordinary, predictions suspect.
Those of us who sink or swim in a vast sea of unknowingness,
expect more from people who hold the future by our hands.
And whether it's curiosity or whim, fear, or even dread
that drives us, there will always be souls fervent for a stranger
to foresee, beneath bulbs burning dim to save electricity,
what fate has in store. We understand that anything can
happen, that life is fraught with danger, a constant struggle
to survive mishap and disease, car accidents and tornados—
can only hope a palmist might prepare us for what comes next.
Tracing Girdles of Venus, Rings of Saturn and Solomon,
lines that signify voyage and travel, marriage and attachment—
palm readers find the future, tell us, if they are kind, you will
marry your true love, live to be an old man, an old woman.
But the pitiless point to lines that show our lovers will betray
us, that we will die young or soon. Either way, we pay—
and where the money goes, only the palmist knows.

CRYSTAL LAKE

Beneath a blue moon, couples at Crystal Lake
lean against each other, swaying—the girls' dresses
pale as Luna moths, their faces aglow—the boys,

holding each partner as if she is blown glass
he is ferrying around the floor. And then the cry
of something wild echoes across the moonlit water,

and the lanterns flicker as if shadows like clouds,
have drifted past them. But they keep dancing:
the girls' glossy heads resting on tuxedoed

shoulders—the boys drawing their dates closer,
clasping them so tight that nothing, not even time,
can pry this moment from their grasp.

SEARCHING FOR SCALLOP SHELLS

for Tommy, 1959 –1980

Searching for scallop shells, my brother and I scoured
the beach, the wind whipping our hair and billowing
our white cotton t-shirts, turning us into salt licks
and nearly blowing us down, we were so small.
But we kept at it, our mother's eyes following us
like twin guard dogs as we went along, her whole
body tense and ready to leap from her lounge chair
at the slightest hint of danger, but letting the usual taut
line between her and us go slack to give us the feel

of freedom. We carried plastic buckets and had them
half-filled in no time since there were hundreds
of scallop shells among the shells whole and broken,
that had washed ashore since we'd been there. How
smooth they were on the inside against our sand-

coated fingertips, and rough on the outside—and they
came in so many colors—purple, orange, gray, burgundy,
calico—shaped just like the Shell sign at the gas station
where our father filled his tank. It was pure joy to find
them, and to know that Grandma was busy cleaning
the fish she'd fry for supper, that soon we'd sit around

the rickety table in our rented cottage with the windows
thrown open and the wind gusting through the bulging
screens with such force, we had to hold our paper
napkins tight in our laps—though it seldom disturbed
the shells on every sill, gripping the wood as if there

were still living creatures inside them. And the grown-
ups' voices, the clatter of silverware, the sighs
of satisfaction, and the pounding waves played music
for our feast as my brother and I nodded over plates piled
high with buttered corn, beefsteak tomatoes, fresh-
caught spot and pompano. And afterward, tired from
the long, hot day, the salty air and the comfortable cocoon
of our family all around us, it didn't take long to fall
asleep—certain that life would always be sweet, like this.

Personal Acknowledgments

For steadfast companionship and unwavering love and support, you can't beat having a relationship with God. So I want to thank Him, first of all, for so many blessings, for never letting us go through tough times alone, and for giving me a sense of humor. Laughter, next to poetry, truly is the best medicine!

Thanks, also, to my daughter, Gia Riana, to whom this collection is lovingly dedicated. You are a strong, brave, and compassionate woman, and I am grateful that both of us survived your teenage years, relatively intact! I love you, darling, and am proud and honored to be your mother.

I couldn't do what I do without my wonderful husband, Leonard, who supports me in every conceivable way, and is just as handsome as he was when I first spotted him in Spanish class at Paisley Middle School, and pretended not to notice.

To my parents, Tom and Loretta Kirby—you are and always have been my best friends. I am so lucky to be your daughter.

To #1 New York Times Best Selling author and Her Royal Highness, THE Sweet Potato Queen, Jill Conner Browne; musician/artist and our favorite Monkee, Peter Tork; composer and educator, Theodore Wiprud; poet, educator, and dear friend, Dr. Felicia Mitchell; my uncle, visual artist Stephen White; beloved syndicated columnist Sharon Randall; and phenomenal photographers Jay Sinclair, Jan Hensley, David Amundson, Dan Rossi, Benita VanWinkle, and Leonard Erickson—thank you for your various contributions to *A Lake of Light and Clouds*. You are all remarkable people. I am in awe of your talent!

Thanks to Susan Nagel Bloch, Mark C. Houston, Frances Y. Dunn, Maricam and Johnny Kaleel, Maureen Sherbondy,

Tim Plowman, Harriet Strickland, Mick Scott, the Smosnas, Debra Hardiman, Debbie Kincaid, the Susans, Fran Kiger, Joanne Henley, Joan Nichols, Jensina and Wendell Burton, Alva Erickson, Stella Gibson, Pamela Byrd, Ron Powers, Linda and Marty Katz, Dr. Shirley Manigault, Elizabeth Reynolds, and countless other teachers, friends, and relatives who have helped, influenced, loved and/or supported me along the way.

To my friend, writer and producer Frank Elliott, for being so justifiably crazy about his lovely wife, Alice!

To friends and relatives no longer with us, including my beloved brother, "Tommy," (Thomas M. Kirby, Jr.), Robert M. Kerr, Guy Neal Williams, Angeline Myers, Folke Erickson, and Vickie Johnson; fellow Cancer Center volunteer Rose Rusch; my grandmothers Ila White and Blanche Fogleman Kirby; grandfathers John Alvin White and John Henry Kirby, Sr.; and great-grandparents Sam and Nannie White. Words can't describe how much they are loved and missed.

To Leroy Moton and the late Viola Gregg Liuzzo, who inspired my poem, "Leroy and Viola," my admiration for their strength and courage in the struggle for Civil Rights knows no bounds. A big thanks to John Railey of the *Winston-Salem Journal* for bringing their story to my attention.

Thank you also, to the A21 Campaign for raising awareness of the scourge of human trafficking. Hopefully, my poem, "Orchid," which won their *Poetry for Their Freedom* contest in 2013, and "Bird," which addresses the same issues, will in some small way, do likewise. For more information about this international organization and their important work, please visit their website at: www.thea21campaign.org.

I'd also like to thank Mrs. Beverly Simstein and her family, for creating *The Simstein Memorial Fund* to honor the memory of Dr. Lee Simstein (remembered for his philanthropic generosity toward patients in need), to help cancer patients in financial distress. I so appreciate the opportunity to donate some of my "poetry money" to this very worthy cause.

To contribute to *The Simstein Memorial Fund*, you can mail your check to: Forsyth Medical Center Foundation, 3333 Silas Creek Parkway, Winston-Salem, NC, 27103. Be sure to indicate that your gift is for the Simstein Fund, and we thank you in advance for your donation. It will help so many people in need.

Thank you to David B. Samadi, MD, Chairman of Urology, Chief of Robotic Surgery at Lenox Hill Hospital, and Professor of Urology at Hofstra North Shore-LIJ School of Medicine in New York City, for saving my husband's life when he had prostate cancer in 2011, and to our friend, M. Gene Bond, PhD, for his invaluable advice and support during this challenging time.

And to the American Cancer Society Hope Lodge Jerome L. Greene Family Center, New York City—thank you for the sanctuary that you offer to cancer patients and their families, and for the kind and courageous friends we met there.

A big thanks, also, to my publisher, Kevin Morgan Watson of Press 53, for the fabulous cover design, for believing in my work, and for our years of friendship. And to Christine Norris, for all of her hard work and dedication to Press 53 and its authors.

And finally, thank you to the editors of every publication that has published my poetry, and to you, dear reader. Consider yourself hugged!

TKE

TERRI KIRBY ERICKSON lives on a quiet cul-de-sac in North Carolina with her husband, Leonard, in a little book- and art-filled ranch house surrounded by songbirds, chipmunks, squirrels, at least one groundhog, and the occasional deer. She is the author of four collections of poetry, including *In the Palms of Angels* (Press 53, 2011), which won a Nautilus Silver Award for Poetry, a Gold Medal for Poetry in the Next Generation Indie Book Awards, and was a Finalist for Poetry in the International Book Awards. Her collection, *Telling Tales of Dusk* (Press 53, 2009) was #23 on the Poetry Foundation Contemporary Best Seller List in 2010.

Her work has appeared in the *2013 Poet's Market*, Ted Kooser's *American Life in Poetry*, *The Christian Science Monitor*, *Verse Daily*, *JAMA*, *North Carolina Literary Review*, *Pirene's Fountain*, *storySouth*, and many others.

She was chosen as the 2013 Leidig Keynote Poet for Emory & Henry College in Virginia, and her poetry has won numerous awards and accolades, most recently the Grand Prize in the *Carolina Woman* Writing Contest and the *Poetry for Their Freedom* award. Since she loves to travel, Terri can often be found roaming the streets of cities both large and small, anywhere from Bloomington, Indiana, to Västerås, Sweden—watching, listening, and remembering—then back home again to write. She is all too aware that squadrons of squirrels eat her birdseed until they roll off the feeders, (bellies bulging), and thus, depend on her book sales for sustenance.

STEPHEN WHITE specializes in figurative paintings done on wood in gold leaf and transparent oil glazes. His work is available through the Little Art Gallery in Raleigh, North Carolina, and Village Smith Gallery in Winston-Salem, North Carolina.

MAR . 2015

CPSIA information can be obtained at www.ICGtesting.com
Printed in the USA
BVOW07s0419050914

365295BV00001B/74/P

9 781941 209028